Treasury of ROMAN LOVE

❖

More *Treasury of Love*
***Poems, Quotations & Proverbs* available:**

Treasury of French Love

Treasury of German Love

Treasury of Italian Love

Treasury of Jewish Love

Treasury of Polish Love

Treasury of Russian Love

Treasury of Spanish Love

Each collection also available as an Audio Book

Hippocrene Books
171 Madison Avenue
New York, NY 10016

Treasury of ROMAN LOVE

❖

Poems, Quotations & Proverbs

In Latin and English

Edited by
Richard A. Branyon

HIPPOCRENE BOOKS
New York

COVER ILLUSTRATION: Banquet Scene from Herculaneum,
Museo Archeologico Nazionale, Naples Italy; courtesy
SCALA/Art Resource, NY.

ISBN 0-7818-0309-8

For information, address:
HIPPOCRENE BOOKS, INC.
171 Madison Avenue
New York, NY 10016

Printed in the United States of America

❖

Contents

LATIN LOVE POEMS

❖

De rerum natura, IV

Haec Venus est nobis; hinc autemst nomen amoris;
hinc illaec primum Veneris dulcedinis in cor
stillavit gutta, et successit frigida cura.
Nam si abest quod ames, praesto simulacra tamen sunt
illius, et nomen dulce obversatur ad auris.
Sed fugitare decet simulacra et pabula amoris
absterrere sibi atque alio convertere mentum
et iacere umorem conlectum in corpora quaeque,
nec retinere, semel conversum unius amore,
et servare sibi curam certumque dolorem;
ulcus enim vivescit et inveterascit alendo,
inque dies gliscit furor atque aerumna gravescit,
si non prima novis conturbes volnera plagis
volgivagaque vagus Venere ante recentia cures
aut alio possis animi traducere motus.
Nec Veneris fructu caret is qui vitat amorem,
sed potius quae sunt sine poena commoda sumit;
nam certe purast sanis magis inde voluptas
quam miseris. Etenim potiundi tempore in ipso
fluctuat incertis erroribus ardor amantem,
nec constat quid primum oculis manibusque fruantur,
quod petier, premunt arte faciuntque dolorem
corporis, et dentes inlidunt saepe labellis
osculaque adfligunt, quia non est pura voluptas
et stimuli subsunt qui instigany laedere id ipsum,
quodcumque est, rabies unde illaec germina surgunt.

Lucretius (98 B.C.-55 B.C)

The Nature of Things, Book 4

This is Venus; this is where love derives its name;
from which the first drop of Venus' sweetness came
and dripped into our hearts, followed by icy anxiety.
For if the object of your love is not there, the images
are there and the sweet name rings sounds in your ears.
The best thing to do is to run away from these images,
to scare off those things that feed on love, and to turn
your mind elsewhere, to cast out the collected fluids
in the body rather than retain it obsessed with the love
of one person only and thus saving up love-sickness
and inevitable pain for yourself; for the sore quickens
and becomes chronic if it is nourished, the madness
gets worse each day and the trouble becomes more
depressing if you do not confound the first wound
with new blows, and cure them while they are fresh by
roaming about engaging in other passionate affairs of
Venus or else transferring your thoughts to another.
Nor does the one who avoids love lack the joy of
sexual passion, on the contrary, he takes the rewards
without paying the penalty; there is no doubt that the
pleasure which comes from this is less contaminated
than it is for pining lovers. For even in the moment of
possession the burning passion of lovers is tossed by
the storms in an uncertain course with no fixed target
for them to enjoy first with eyes or hands. They press
closely their desired object and cause physical pain,
they often bite into the lips in the violent collision of
a kiss because their pleasure is contaminated and
instincts lurk to compel them to hurt the very thing,
whatever it is, from which this dark madness grows.

❖

De rerum natura, IV

Sed tamen esto iam quantovis oris honore,
cui Veneris membris vis omnibus exoriatur:
nempe aliae quoque sunt; nempe hac sine viximus ante;
nempe eadem facit, et scimus facere, omnia turpi,
et miseram taetris se suffit odoribus ipsa,
quam famulae longe fugitant furtimque cachinnant.
At lacrimans exclusus amator limina saepe
floribus et sertis operit postisque superbos
unguit amaracino et foribus miser oscula figit;
quem si, iam ammissum, venientem offenderit aura
una modo, causas abeundi quaerat honestas,
et meditata diu cadat alte sumpta querella,
plus videat quam mortali concedere par est.
Nec Veneres nostras hoc fallit; quo magis ipsae
omnia summo opere hos vitae postscaenia celant
quos retinere volunt adstrictosque esse in amore,
nequiquam, quoniam tu animo tamen omnia possis
protrahere in lucem atque omnis inquirere risus,
et, si bello animost et non odiosa, vicissim
praetermittere et humanis concedere rebus.

Lucretius

❖

The Nature of Things, Book 4

Even so, however respectable her face, even of the power of Venus streams out of all her limbs, there are still other women; we managed to live without her before; she does just the same things as other women do, anointing herself with disgusting odors, causing her maids to run about and giggle behind her back. But the tearful locked-out lover keeps covering her threshold with flowers and garlands, anointing the door posts with sweet marjoram and planting his kisses on the door; but if he is let inside, once he get one sniff of the air, there would be an end to his well-rehearsed poem drawn from his heart; then he would curse himself for being so stupid as to credit her with qualities more than mortal. Our
women
are quite aware of this, so they are at great pains to hide from those whom they wish to keep bound in the chains of love. But all is vanity, since you can in your minds drag them out into day and seek the cause of their laughing. Then, if the woman is kind-hearted and not given to spite you could turn a blind eye and make allowances for such human weaknesses.

❖

Carmina V

Vivamus, mea Lesbia, atque amemus,
rumoresque senum seueriorum
omnes unius aestimemus assis!
Soles occidere et redire possunt;
nobis cum semel occidit breuis lux,
nox est perpetua una dormienda.
Da mi basia mille, deinde centum,
deinde mille altera, dein secunda centum,
deinde usque altera mille, deinde centum.
Dein, cum milia multa facerimus,
conturbabimus illa, ne sciamus,
aut ne quis malus inuidere possit,
cum tantum sciat esse basiorum.

Catullus (84 B.C.-54 B.C.)

❖

Poem 5

My Lesbia, let us live and love
And care not the least for old men
Who sermonize and disapprove.
Suns when they sink can rise again,
But we, when our brief light has shone,
Must sleep through the long night.
Kiss me a thousand kisses, then
A hundred more, then a second
Thousand and hundred, and now
Thousands and hundreds more
And we lose count of how many
And nobody can do evil to us
By keeping count of our kisses.

❖

Carmina VII

Quaeris, quot mihi bastiationes
tuae, Lesbia, sint satis superque.
Quam magnus numerus Libyssae harenae
lasarpiciferis iacet Cyrenis
oraculum Iovis inter aestuosi
et Batti veteris sacrum sepulcrum;
aur quam sidera multa, cum tacet nox,
furtiuos hominum vident amores:
tam te basia multa basiare
vesano satis et super Catullo est,
quae nec pernumerare curiosi
possint nec mala fascinare lingua.

Catullus

❖

Poem 7

You ask me how may kisses satisfy
You Lesbia, how many are enough.
As many as the grains of sand in Libya
Sprinkling the shores of Cyrene,
Between the shrine of Jupiter
And the tomb of old King Battus,
As many as the stars above, in silent night
Shine upon the secrets of men's loves.
When he has this many kisses
Catullus will have slaked his appetite,
So many kisses that the curious crowd
Are not able to speak words of spite.

❖

Carmina VIII

Miser Catulle, desinas ineptire,
et quod vides perisse perditum ducas,
fulsere quondam candidi tibi soles,
cum ventitibas quo puella ducebat
amata nobis quantum amabitur nulla.
Ibi illa multa tum iocosa fiebant,
quae tu volebas nec puella nolebat,
fulsere vere candidi tibi soles.
Nunc iam illa non vult; tu quoque impotens, noli,
nec quae fugit sectare, nec miser vive
sed obstinata mente perfer, obdura.
Vale, puella. Iam Catullus obdurat,
nec te requiret nec rogabit inuitam,
at tu dolebis, cum rogaberis nulla.
Scelesta, vae te, quae tibi manet vita?
quis nunc te adibit? Cui videberis bella?
quem nunc amabis? Cuius esse diceris?
quem basiabis? Cui labella mordebis?
at tu, Catulle, destinatus obdura.

Catullus

❖

Poem 8

Miserable Catullus stop being foolish
And admit that what can see is lost.
The sun was shining in those days
When you gave your girl such a love
That nobody else will ever have.
Those were the days of lovers' games
When she gave you anything you wanted;
That was a time when the sun truly shone.
But now she is cold and does not want me;
Weak as you are you must not be miserable
Be obstinate and resign yourself to accept it.
Goodbye my girl, Catullus is adamant now,
He no longer needs your favors and kisses,
You will feel the pain when no one needs you.
You bitch, what will life hold for you then?
Who will visit you? Who will say you're pretty?
Whom will you love? Who will say they own you?
Whom will you kiss? Whose lips will you nibble?
And you Catullus, stand firm and be like a stone.

Carmina LXX

Nulli se dicit mulier mea nubere malle
quam mihi, non si se Iuppiter petat.
Dicit: sed mulier cupido dicit amanti,
un vento et rapida scribere oportet aqua.

Carmina LXXII

Dicebas quondam solum te nosse Catullum,
Lesbia, nec prae me velle tenere Iovem.
Dilexi tum te non tantum ut vulgus amicam,
sed pater ut gnatos diligit et generos.
Nunc te cognovi: quare etsi impensius uror,
multo mi tamen es vilior et levior.
Qui potis est, inquis? Quod amantem iniuria talis
cogit amare magis, sed bene velle minus.

Carmina LXXXVI

Quintia formosa est multis, mihi candida, longa,
recta est: haec ego sic singula confiteor.
Totum illud formosa nego: nam nulla venustas,
nulla in tam magno est corpore mica salis.
Lesbia formosa est, quae cum pulcherrima tota est,
tum omnibus una omnis surripuit Veneres.

Carmina LXXXVII

Nulla potest mulier tantum se dicere amatam
vere, quantum a me Lesbia amata mea est.
Nulla fides ullo fuit umquam in foedere tanta,
quanta in amore tuo parte mea est.

Catullus

Poem 70

She swears that she would rather marry me
Than anyone, even if Jupiter himself were courting.
She swears, but what a girl swears to her lover
Ought to be scribbled on winds and on water.

Poem 72

You used to say Lesbia, that you were mine
And called me more desirable than Jove.
I loved you then not as a vulgar friend
But as a father cares for his children.
Now that I know you, almost as a wife
You have become much more vile and light.
You ask how can that be? In love deceit
Freezes affection but increases passion.

Poem 86

Many think that Quintia is beautiful. She is tall,
Straight and has lovely white skin; I grant these
Good points, but she has one fault: no sexuality.
There is not a grain of salt in her dish to excite.
Lesbia is beautiful, more beautiful than all others,
Dressed in a mystery she has stolen from Venus.

Poem 87

No woman can truthfully say to her lover
That any man ever loved her as I love you.
No lover bound by the most sacred pledge
Was ever found more true to his love.

Aeneid IV (1-30)

At regina gravi iamdudum saucia cura
vulnus alit venis et caeco carpitur igni.
Multa viri virtus animo multusque recursat
gentis honos; haerent infixi pectore vultus
verbaque, nec placidam membris dat cura quietam.
Postera Phoeba lustrabat lampade terras
umentemque Aurora polo dimoverat umbram,
cum sic unanimam adloquitur male sana sonorem:
"Anna soror, quae me suspensam insomnia terrent!
quis novus hic nostris successit sedibus hospes,
quem sese ore ferens, quam forti pectore et armis!
Credo equidem, nec vana fides, genus esse deorum.
Degeneres animos timor arguit. Heu quibus ille
iactatus fatis! Quae bella exhausta candebat!
Si mihi non animo fixum immotumque sederet,
ne cui me vinclo vellem sociare iugali,
postquam primus amor deceptam morte fefellit;
si non pertaesum thalami taedaeque fuisset,
huic uni forsan potui succumbere culpae.
Anna, fatebor enim, miseri post fata Sychaei
coniugis et sparsos fraterna caede Penatis
solus hic inflexit sensus animumque labantem
impulit. Adnosco veteris vestigia flammae.
Sed mihi vel tellus optem prius ima dehiscat
vel pater omnipotens adigat me fulmine ad umbras,
pallentis umbras Erebo noctemque profundam,
ante, Pudor, quam te volo aut tua iura resolvo.
Ille meos, primus qui me sibi iunxit, amores
abstulit; ille habeat secum servetque sepulchro."
Sic effata sinum lacrimus implevit obortis.

Virgil (70 B.C.-19 B.C.)

❖

Aeneid, Book 4 (1-30)

But the queen, who had been smitten with an
incurable love-pang, feeds the wound with her
life-blood and is wasted away with unseen fire.
Her heart often rushes back to her chief's valor,
his glorious heritage, his looks and words stick fast
to her bosom but the pang remains in all her limbs.
The new day's dawn was lighting the earth with
lamp of Apollo and had already scattered from
the sky the dewy shades, when much distraught,
she speaks to her sister, her sole confidante.
"Anna, my sister, what dreams fill me with fears!
Who is the stranger that hath entered our home?
How noble his manner! How brave in heart and arms!
I believe it well, that he is sprung from the gods.
Fear alone proves creatures to be common.
Alas! What amazing fates perplex his soul!
What wars, long endured, does he recount!
If I had not sworn to myself to be fixed and
immovable, to bond with none in wedlock,
since my first lover turned traitor and cheated
me by death, were I not weary of the bridal bed
and torch, I might have yielded to this chance.
Anna, for I admit it, since the death of Syncheus,
and destruction of our home by a brother's murder,
he has swayed my will and overthrown my soul.
I recognize the traces of the old flame. I would
rather pray, may the depths of earth yawn for me,
or may the almighty father strike me with his bolt
to the shades, the abysmal darkness of Erebus,
before, O Shame, I violate you and your laws.
He, who was my first love, has taken my heart;
may he keep it with him and guard it in the grave!"
Saying this, she filled her bosom with tears.

❖

Aeneid IV (54-86)

His dictis incensum animum inflammavit amore
spemque dedit dubiae menti solvitque pudorem.
Principio delubra adeunt pacemque per aras
exquirunt; mactant lectas de more bidentis
legiferae Cereri Phoeboque patrique Lyaeo,
Iunonio ante omnis, cui vincla iugalia curae;
ipsa tenens dextra pateram pulcherrima Dido
candentis vaccae media inter cornua fundit
aut ante ora deum pinguis spatiatur ad aras,
instauratque diem donis, pecudumque eclusis
pectoribus inhians spirantia consulit esta.
Heu vatum ignarae mentes! Quid vota furentum,
quid delubra iuvant? Est mollis flamma medullas
interea et tacitum vivit sub pectore vulnus.
Uritur infelix Dido totaque vagatur
urbe furens, qualis coniecta cerva sagitta,
quam procul incautam nemora inter Cresia fixit
pastor agens telis liquitque volatile ferrum
nescius; illa fuga silvas saltusque peragrat
Dictaeos; haeret lateri letalis harundo.
Nunc media Aenean secum per moenia ducit
Sidoniasque ostentat opes urbemque paratam;
incipit effari, mediaque in voce resistit;
nunc eadem labente die convivia quaerit,
Iliacosque iterum demens audire labores
exposcit pendetque iterum narrantis ab ore.

❖

Aeneid, Book 4 (54-86)

With these words she fanned into flames the
love in the queen's heart and placed hope in
her uncertain mind, freeing the bonds of shame.
First they visit the shrines and pray for peace
at each altar, and they slay the best sheep for
Ceres the law-giver, for Phoebus and father
Lyaeus and for Juno, guardian of marriage.
Dido herself, without equal in beauty, with cup
in hand, pours the libations between the horns
of a white heifer, and before the gods, walks
to the rich altars and makes solemn that day
with gifts; then peering into the dying breasts
of the sacrificed creatures, foresees the future.
Oh, blind soul of prophets! What avail are the
vows and shrines to one smitten with wild love?
All the while the flame engulfs her tender heart
and deep in her breast lives the silent wound.
Unhappy Dido burns and though everyone in
the city below wanders about in disorder, just
as the hind, wounded with an arrow from afar
in the Cretan woods by an unwary shepherd,
leaving in her the burning steel: she runs through
Dictaean woods with the deadly shaft in her side.
Now she leads Aeneas throughout the city and
displays her Sidonian wealth; she tries to speak
but stops with half-spoken words. As the day
turns into evening she retires to the banquet
and again longs to hear the woes of Ilium and
to linger over each word on the speaker's lips.

Post ubi digressi, lumenque obscura vicissim
luna premit suadentque cadentia sidera somnos,
sola domo maeret vacua stratisque relictis
incubat. Illum absens absentem auditque videtque,
aut gremio Ascanium, genitoris imagine capta,
detinet, infandum si faller possit amorem.

Virgil

When everyone has gone and the dim moon sinks into the night, and the stars appear, she mourns alone in the empty room and falls on the couch he has left. Though he is absent, she hears him, she sees him, and captivated by his father's looks, she holds Ascanius on her lap, so that she may savor a passion beyond description.

❖

Carmina I, V

Quis multa gracilis te puer in rosa
perfusus liquidis urget odoribus
grato, pyrrha, sub antro?
cui flavum religas comam,

Simplex munditiis? Leu quotiens fidem
mutatosque deos flebit et aspera
nigris aequora ventis
emirabitur insolens,

Qui nunc te fruitur credulus aurea,
qui semper vacuam, semper amabilem
sperat, nescius aurae
fallacis. Miseri, quibus

Intemptata nites. Me tabula sacer
votiva paries indicat uvida
suspendisse potenti
vestimenta maris deo.

Horace (65 B.C.-8 B.C.)

❖

Book 1, Ode 5

What slender youth, covered with perfumes
Embraces you among the myriad roses
In the pleasant grotto, O Pyrrha?
For who do you tie up your hair

With such simple elegance? How often
Shall he lament the fickle faith and gods,
And wonder at rough waters in a stormy gale,
He who now embraces you,

As he fondly sees you in a golden aura,
Who hopes that you will be free of passion
For another, and always beautiful, ignorant
He who knows not the treacherous breeze.

Wretched ones to whom you, untried, now
Appear so dazzling. As for me, the temple
With its votive tablet shows I have hung up
My garments to the god, master of the sea.

Carmina I, XIII

Cum tu, Lydia, Telephi
cervicem roseam, cerea Telephi
laudas bracchia, vae, meum
fervens difficli bile tumet iecur.

Tunc nec mens mihi nec color
certa sede manet, umor et in genas
furtim labitur, arguens
quam lentis penitus macerer ignibus.

Uror, seu tibi candidos
turparunt umeros immodicae mero
rixae, sive puer furens
impressit memorem dente labris notam.

Non, si me satis audias,
spere perpetuum dulcia barbare
laedentem oscula, quae Venus
quinta parte sui nectaris imbuit.

Felices ter et ampluis,
quos irrupta tenet copula nec malis
divulsus querimoniis
suprema citius solvet amor die.

Horace

❖

Book 1, Ode 13

When you, O Lydia, praise
the rosy neck of Telephus,
or his waxen arms, my heart
swells with an angry passion.

My senses take leave of reason
and my complexion pales, while
a moist tear glides down my cheek
proving the lingering fires of my love.

I burn to think how, mad with wine,
that boy has harmed your gleaming
shoulders, or in a state of frenzy he
left his teeth marks on your lips.

If you had heeded me, you would not
hoped for constancy from that one
who savagely profanes the sweet lips
that Venus has imbued with nectar.

Three times blessed and more are they
who are united with an unbroken bond;
no wretched quarrels shall ever separate
our love before the final days of life.

❖

Carmina I, XXIII

Vitas hinnuleo me similis, Chloe,
quaerenti pavidam montibus aviis
matrem non sine vano
aurarum et siluae metu.

Nam se mobilibus veris inhorruit
adventus foliis, seu virides rubum
dimovere lacertae,
et corde et genibus tremit.

Atqui non ego te tigris ut aspera
Gaqetulusve leo frangere persequor:
tandem desine matrem
tempestiva sequi viro.

Horace

❖

Book 1, Ode 23

You shy away from me Chloe like a young
deer lost in the mountains, looking for its
mother, frightened by the gentle breeze
in the trees and creatures in the forest.

With the leaves blowing in the shadows
and in the fresh wind of springtime, and
brambles at her feet, she quivers and
her knees and heart grow faint.

Yet my purpose is not to crush you
like some savage tiger or wild lion.
Stop following your mother's steps,
since it is time for you to have a man.

❖

Carmina I, XXV

Parcius iunctas quatiunt fenestras
ictibus crebris iuvenes protervi,
nec tibi comnos adimunt, amatque
ianua limen,

Quae prius multum facilis movebat
cardines. Audis minus et minus iam:
"me tuo longas pereunte noctes,
Lydia, dormis?"

Invicem moechos anus arrogantis
flebis in solo levis angiportu,
Thracio bacchante magis sub
interlunia vento,

Cum tibi flagrans amor et libido,
quae solet matres furiare equorum,
saeviet circa iecur ulcerosum,
non sine questu,

Laeta quod pubes hedera virenti
gaudeat pulla magis atque myrto,
aridas frondis hiemis sodali
dedicet Euro.

Horace

❖

Book 1, Ode 25

Less often now do youths shake your windows
With repeated blows, no longer do they steal
Their slumbers from you, and the door
To your room is now often closed

That once moved so freely on its hinges.
Less and less often do you hear such utterances:
"How can you sleep my dearest Lydia, while I,
your lover die out here in the long night?"

Your turn will come you arrogant bitch
And you will become a lone hag in a deserted alley
You shall weep over your lover's sorrows on some
Moonless night with the Thracian wind blowing,

While your burning love and passions
Like those of a wild stallion before a mare,
Shall rage about your wounded heart
And fester inside you without ceasing.

Then you shall moan the merry youths
That take delight in the ivy green and myrtle
While you are consigned to withered leaves
Of the east wind, the winter's mate.

❖

Carmina II, I

Adde merum vinoque novos compesce dolores,
occupet ut fessi lumina victa spor;
neu quisquam multo percussum tempora Baccho
excitet, infelix dum requiescit amor:
nam posita est nostrae custodia saeva puellae,
clauditur et dura ianua firma sera.

Ianua difficilis domini, te verberet imber,
te Iovis imperio fulmina missa petant.
Ianua, iam pateas uni mihi, victa querelis,
neu furtim verso cardine aperta sones;
et mala siqua tibi dixit dementia nostra,
ignoscas: capiti sint precor illa meo.
Te meminisse decet quae plurima voce peregi
supplice, cum posti florida serta darem.

Tu quoque, ne timide custodes, Delia, falle;
audendum est: fortes adiuuat ipsa Venus.
Illa favet seu quis iuvenis nova limina temptat
seu reserat fixo dente puella fores.
Illa docet molli furtim derepere lecto,
illa pedem nullo ponere posse sono,
illa viro coram nutus conferre loquaces
blandaque compositis abdere verba notis;
nec docet hoc omnes sed quos nec inertia tardat
nec vetat obscura surgere nocte timor.

Tibullus (55 B.C.-19 B.C.)

❖

Book 2, Poem 1 (1-24)

Pour the wine, drive away the new misery,
and let sleep invade my tired defeated eyes.
And when the strength of Bacchus hits my brain
see that no one wakes me while I am at rest,
for now a cruel guard stands watch over my girl
and her heavy door is shut and firmly locked.

O door, stubborn as your master, may the storm
destroy you, may the flash of Jove's lightning blast you.
Please door, open for me, moved by my baneful cries,
but you are silent as you swing on your slow hinge.
Forgive me if I cursed you in my infatuation.
Let the curses fall upon my own head. You
should remember all my prayers and promises
when I hung those garlands on your posts.

And you, Delia: be bold and trick the guard.
You must take action, for Venus favors the brave.
She favors the young man who waits at the threshold
and the girl who opens the door with a home-made key.
She teaches the girl to slip out of a soft bed in secrecy,
how to walk across the floor without making a sound,
how to glance at her lover in presence of her husband,
how to conceal sweet words with secret signals.
Her teaching is not for everyone but only those
with courage to rise in the shadow of the night.

❖

Carmina II, IV (1-26)

Sic mihi seruitium video dominamque paratum:
iam mihi, libertas illa paterna, vale.
Seruitium sed triste datur, teneaorque catenis,
et numquam misero vincla remittit Amor,
et seu quid merui seu mil peccavimus, urit.
Uror: io, remoue, saeva puella, faces.

O ego ne possim tales sentire dolores,
quam mallem in gelidis montibus esse lapis!
Stare vel insanis cautes obnoxia ventis,
naufraga et amara dies et noctis amarior umbra est;
omnia nunc tristi tempora felle madent.
Nec prosent elegi nec carminis auctor Apollo:
illa cava pretium flagitat usque manu.

Ite procul, Musae, si non prodestis amanti:
non ego vos ut sint bello canenda colo,
nec refero Solisque vias et qualis, ubi orbem
compleuit, versis Luna recurrit equis.
Ad dominam faciles aditus per carmina quaero:
ite procul, Musae, si nihil ista valent.

At mihi per caedem et facinus sunt dona paranda,
ne iaceam calusam flebilis ante domum.
Aut rapiam suspensa sacris insignia fanis:
sed Venus ante alios est violenada mihi.
Illa malum facinus suadat dominamque rapacem
dat mihi: sacrilegas illa manus.

Tibullus

❖

Book 2, Poem 4 (1-26)

I see slavery to a mistress closing on me;
Goodbye now to the freedom of my fathers.
I accept the most cruel bondage, for I am held
Chained and never does Love relax its bond.
He burns me and even though I am not to blame
I am burning now, oh girl, remove the torch.

I need never to experience this torment
I would rather be a stone on a cold mountain
Or a savage crag exposed to violent gales
Buffeted by the sea's thundering waves.
The day is bitter, still more bitter is the night;
Every moment is soaked with tearful remorse.
The elegies of Phoebus, patron of the poets,
Are of no help; my lady demands more money.

Leave me alone Muses, if you cannot help a lover.
I do not ask your help in singing of distant wars
Not do I watch the Sun-God or tell how the Moon,
Once her orbit completed, turns her horses back.
By poetry I look for easy access to a mistress.
Leave me alone, O Muses, if your magic fails.

I must take crime and bloodshed to obtain her gifts
That save me from those sorrowful vigils at her door;
Or steal the sacred offerings hung on the temple walls;
But Venus will be the first goddess to be profaned.
She tempts me to do evil and devotes me to a
Greedy mistress; she deserves to suffer sacrilege.

❖

Carmina II, II

Liber eram et vacuo meditabar vivere lecto;
at me composita pace fefellit Amor.
Cur haec in terris facies humana moratur?
Iuppiter, ignosco pristina furta tua.

Fulva coma est longaeque manus, et maxima toto
corpore, et incedit vel Iove digna soror,
aut cum Munychias Pallas spatiatur as aras,
Gorgonis anguiferae pectus operta comis;
aut patrio qualis ponit verstigia ponto
mille Venus teneris cincta Cupidinibus.

Cedite iam, divae, quas pastor viderat olim
Idaeis tunicas ponere verticibus!
Hanc utinam faciem nolit mutare senectus,
etsi Cumaeae saecula vatis aget!

Propertius 50 B.C.-16 B.C.)

❖

Book 2, Poem 2

Free was I, intending to live in a single bed;
but in making my peace Love betrayed me.
Why does such beauty linger among mortals?
Jove, I pardon your secret loves of old.

She has auburn hair and slender hands; her
tall figure is regal; her walk is worthy of Jove,
Like Pallas she steps up to the Athenian altars,
her breasts covered with a Gorgon's chevelure;
or like Venus attended by a thousand Cupids,
setting foot upon the sea that gave her birth.

Stand aside, goddesses whom the shepherd
saw disrobe on the high peaks of Ida long ago.
May old age refuse to transform her beauty,
even if she becomes old as Cumae's Sibyl.

❖

Carmina II, VIII (1-16)

Eripitur nobis iam pridem cara puella:
et tu me lacrimas fundere, amice, vetas?
nullae sunt inimicitiae nisi amoris acerbae:
ipsum me iugula, lenior hostis ero.

Possum ego in alterius positam spectare lacerto?
nec mea dicetur, quae modo dicta meast?
omnia vertuntur: certe vertuntut amores:
vinceris aut victis, haec in amore rota est.

Magni saepe duces, magni cedidere tyranni,
et Thebae steterunt ataque Troia fuit.
Munera quanta dedi vel qualia carmina feci!
Illa tamen numquam ferrea dixit "amo."

Ergo ego tam multos nimium temerarius annos,
improba, qui tulerim teque tuamque domum?
ecquandone tibi liber sum visus? An usque
in nostrum iacies verba superba caput?

Propertius

❖

Book 2, Poem 8 (1-16)

She is gone, the dear girl that I loved so long,
And you, my friend, you don't even shed a tear?
No hatred is bitter compared with a lover's woe:
Slay me now and I will find you less despicable.

How can I bear to see her held in the arms of another?
She is no longer called mine, though she was just now.
All things change, and love changes with them: You lose
To those you conquered, thus spins of the wheel of love.

Many great generals and tyrants have been conquered,
Thebes is destroyed and lofty Troy exists no longer.
What presents I gave her, what poems composed!
Yet never did she say "I love you." She is cold as iron.

So all these years I have been foolish, have I woman?
I supported you and everyone in our household.
Did you ever treat me as a man with rights?
Will you always cast insults to my face?

❖

Carmina II, XII

Quiccumque ille fuit, puerum qui pinxit Amorem,
nonne putas miras hunc habuisse manus?
is primum vidit sine sensu viver amantis,
et levibus curis magna perire bona.
Idem non rustra ventosas addidat alas,
fecit et humano corde volare deum:
scilicet atlerna quoniam iactamur in unda,
nostraque non ullis permanet aura locis.
Et merito hamatis manus est armata sagittis,
et pharetra ex umero Cnosia utroque iacet:
ante ferit quaniam tuti quam cernimus hostem,
nec quisquam ex illo vulnere sanus abit.

In me tela manent, manet et puerilis imago:
sed certe pennas perdidit ille suas;
evolat heu nostro quoniam de pectore nusquam,
assiduusque meo sanguine bella gerit.
Quid tibi iucundum est siccis habitare medullis?
si pudor est, alio traice tela, puer!
Intactos isto satius temptare veneno:
non ego, sed tenuis vapulat umbra mea.
Quam si perdideris, quis erit qui talia cantet,
(haec mea Muse levis gloria magna tua est)
qui caput et digitos et lumina nigra puellae
et canat ut soleant molliter ire pedes?

Propertius

❖

Book 2, Poem 12

Whoever painted Cupid as a young boy,
don't you think he had a wonderful talent?
He was the first to see that lovers are children,
and that great happiness is lost by petty passion.
With good reason he added fluttering wings
and made the god fly into the human heart:
since we are often tossed by the winds of love
and the wind never remains in the same quarter.
And appropriately he is armed with barbed arrows,
and a Cretan quiver is suspended from his shoulder,
since he strikes when we feel safe and never see him,
and from that wound no one ever departs unscathed.

His arrows are still with me, and his youthful visage;
but he has certainly lost his wings, since nowhere
from my heart does he fly away, but at great cost
of my blood continues to wage eternal war.
What pleasure do you gain from such an action?
For shame boy, shoot your arrows elsewhere!
Better to attack those who have never felt the
poison of your arrows: it is not me, but only a
poor shadow of my former self that you punish.
If you destroy me who will sing your praises
(for my slight Muse is your greatest fame),
who will sing of my girl's face, her hands,
her dark eyes and how daintily she walks?

❖

Carmina II, XV (1-12)

O me felicem! Nox o mihi candida! Et o tu
lectule deliciis facte beate meis!
Quam multa apposita narramus verba lucerna,
quantaque sublato lumine fuit!

Nam modo nudatis mecum est luctata papillis,
interdum tunica duxit operta moram.
Illa meos somno lapsos patefecit ocellos
ore suo et dixit "sicine, lente, iaces?"

Quam vario amplexu mutamus bracchia! Quantum
oscula sunt labris nostra morata tuis!
Non iuvat in caeco Venerem corrumpere motu:
si nescis, oculi sunt in amore duces.

Propertius

❖

Book 2, Poem 15 (1-16)

O happy me! O night has shone for me! And O you
my darling bed made blessed by my delight.
What happy words we shared beside the lamp
And how happily we struggled when the light was out!

For now she wrestled me with her bare breasts
And closed her tunic and teased me with delay.
With a kiss she opened my eyes, heavy with sleep,
And whispered, "How can you sleep, lazybones!"

How often our arms slipped into new embraces.
How long my kisses lingered on her sweet lips.
Venus is spoiled by serving her in darkness,
Surely you know that sight is the path of love.

❖

Carmina II, XXIVb

Hoc erat in primis quod me gaudere iubebas?
tam te formosam non pudet esse levem?
una aut altera nox nondum est in amore peracta,
et dicor lecto iam gravis esse tuo.
Me modo laudabas et carmina nostra legebas:
ille tuus pennas tam cito vertit amor?
dirast quae multis simulatum fingit amorem,
et se plus uni si qua parare potest.

Contendat mecum ingenio, contendat et arte,
in primis una discat amare domo:
si libitum tibi erit, Lernaeas pugnet ad hydras
et tibi ab Hesperio mala dracone ferat,
taetra venena libens et naufragus ebibat undas,
et numquam pro te deneget esse miser:
quos utinam in nobis, vita, experiare labores!
Iam tibi de timidis iste protervus erit,
qui nunc se in tumidum iactando venit honorem:
discidium vobis proximus annus erit.
At me non aetas mutabit tota Sibyllae,
non labor Alcidae, non niger ille dies.
Tum me compones et dices ossa, Properti.
Haec tua sunt: eheu tu mihi certus eras,
certus eras eheu, quamvis nec sanguine avito
nobilis et quamvis non ita dives eras.
Nil ego non patiar, numquam me iniuria mutat:
ferre ego formosam nullum onus esse puto
credo ego non paucos ista periisse figura,
credo ego sed multos non habuisse fidem.

Propertius

❖

Book 2, Poem 24B

Was it for this that you wished me to be happy?
Are you not ashamed to be so beautiful and so
fickle at the same time? We only spent one or
two nights together and already you tell me that
I am not welcome in your bed. Just as you sung
my praises and read my poems, has your love so
quickly turned its fickle wings elsewhere? Cruel
is the woman who professes her false love to many
and is so bold to give her charms to more than one.

Let another man compete with me in art and craft,
and learn to confine his love to a single woman:
if you wish, let him fight the Lernaean hydras and
bring you apples from the serpent of the Hesperides;
let him drink the poison waters from the shipwreck,
and never shirk suffering for your sake, oh that you
might test me in such ordeals! And soon you will see
your hero become a coward, because his boasts have
brought him false honor, within a year you will part.
But a whole lifetime of the Sibyl will not change my
love, nor the labors of Hercules, nor blackest death.
Then you will bury me and say "Here lie your bones,
Propertius, Alas, you were faithful to me, although
the son of an ignoble family and not prosperous."
There is nothing that I cannot endure for your sake;
pain and suffering never change my love: I do not
consider it a hardship to bear for one so beautiful.
I believe that many have been smitten by such
beauty, but very few have remained true.

❖

Amores I, IV

Vir tuus est epulas nobis aditurus easdem—
ultima coena tuo sit, precor, illa viro!
Ergo ego dilectam tantum conviva puellam
adsciciam? Tangi quem iuvet, alter erit,
alteriusque sinus apte subiecta fovebis?
iniciet collo, cum volet, ille manum?
desine mirari, posito quod candida vino
Atracis ambiguos traxit in arma viros.
Nec mehi silva domus, nec equo mea membra cohaerent.
Vix a te videor posse tenere manus!
Quae tibi sint facienda tamen cognosce, nec Euris
da mea nec tepidis verba ferenda Notis!
Ante veni, quam vir—nec quid, si veneris ante,
possit agi video; sed tamen ante veni.
Cum premet ille torum, vultu comes ipsa odesto
ibis, ut accumbas—clam mihi tange pedem!
Me specta nutusque meos vultumque loquacem;
excipe furtivas et refer ipsa notas.
Verba superciliis sine voce loquentia dicam;
verba leges digitis, verba notata mero.
Cum tibi succurret Veneris lascivia nostrae,
purpureas tenero pollice tange genas.
Si quid erit, de me tacita quod mente queraris
pendeat extrema mollis ab aure manus.
Cum tibi, quae faciam, mea lux, dicamve, placebunt,
versetur digitis anulus usque tuis.
Tange manu mensam, tangunt quo more precantes,
optabis merito cum mala multa viro.

Ovid (43 B.C.-A.D. 17)

❖

Amores I, 4

Your husband will attend the same banquet with us—
I pray that this would be the last dinner for him.
Must I then look at the girl I love as a mere guest?
Does the joy of feeling your touch belong to another
and must it be upon his breast you choose to recline?
Shall he put his arm around you whenever he wishes?
I no longer marvel that when the wine had been poured
the fair daughter of Atrax drove the Centaurs to combat.
My home is not in the forest, nor are my limbs part-man
and part-horse, but I can hardly keep my hands off you.
Now learn what your task must be; do not give my words
to the East wind to be blown away, or to the South wind.
Arrive before your husband—and yet I do not see what
can be done if you arrive before, but so this anyway.
When he sits on the couch, you will come with your
modest demeanor and sit beside him—in secret give
my foot a touch! Keep your eyes on me, to see my
nods and the language of my eyes and catch my
secret love signs so you may secretly return them.
With my brows I shall say to you words that speak
without sound, you will read words from my fingers,
you will read words traced in the wine glass.
When you think of the wanton pleasure of our
passion, touch your rosy cheeks with your finger.
If you have in mind a slight grievance against me,
let your hand touch the lowest part of your ear.
When my actions please you, light of my life,
keep turning your ring about your finger.
Lay your hand upon the table as those who
place their hands in silent prayer, when you
wish your husband the evils that he deserves.

❖

Amores I, V

Aestus erat, mediamque dies exegerat horam;
adposui medio membra levanda toro.
Pars adaperta fuit, pars altera clausa fenestrae;
quale fere silvae lumen habere solent,
qualia sublucent fugiente crepuscula Phoebo,
aut ubi nox abiit, nec tamen orta dies.
Illa verecundis lux est praebenda puellis,
qua timidus latebras speret habere pudor.
Ecce, Corinna venit, tunica velata recincta,
candida dividua colla tegente coma—
qualiter in thalamos famosa Semiramis isse
dicitur, et multis Lais amata viris.
Deripui tunicam—nec multam rara nocebat;
pugnabat tunica sed tamen illa tegi.
Quae cum ita pugnaret, tamquam quae vincere nollet,
victa est non aegre proditione sua.
Ut stetit ante oculos posito velamine nostros,
in toto nusquam coropore menda fuit.
Quos umeros, quales vidi tetigique lacertos!
Forma papillarum quam fuit apta premi!
Quam castigato planus sub pectore venter!
Quantum et quale latus! Quam iuvenale femur!
Singula quid referam? Nil non laudabile vidi
et nudam pressi corpus ad usque meum.
Cetera quis nescit? Lassi requievimus ambo.
Proveniant medii sic saepe dies!

Ovid

❖

Amores I, 5

It was just past noon on a sultry summer day;
I laid my limbs to rest in the middle of my couch.
One shutter of my window was open, the other closed;
the light in the room was as soft as the dim forest, or as
the faint glow of twilight when Phoebus is taking leave,
or when night has gone and the morning has not come.
It was such a light as bashful maids should have whose
timid modesty hopes to hide them away from the world.
Behold, Corinna comes, draped in a girded tunic,
with divided hair falling over her fair, white neck—
such as the hair of Semiramis in her bridal
chamber, or that of Lais, loved by many men.
I tore away the tunic—it was fine and scarcely
took away from her charms; but she struggled
to keep her tunic on. Even while she fought as one
who would not be overcome, she lost by her own
betrayal. As she stood before my eyes with her
tunic aside, there was no sign of fault on her body.
What shoulders, what arms I saw, what a sensation!
Her breasts were perfectly suited for my caress.
How smooth was her body beneath her bosom!
What a long, beautiful side. How fair her thighs!
Why recount each charm? I saw nothing that was
not worthy of praise; I clasped her body to mine.
The rest, who does not know? Worn out, we
both lay in quiet repose. May my fortune bring
many more middays as wonderful as this one.

❖

Amores II, V (1-32)

Nullus amor tanti est—abeas, pharetrate Cupido—
ut mihi sint totiens maxima vota mori.
Vota mori mea sunt, cum te pecasse recordor,
o mihi perpetuum nata puella malum!
Non male dletae nudant tua facta tabellae,
nec data furtive munera crimen habent.
O utinam arguerem sic, ut non vincere possem!
Me miserum! Quare tam bona causa mea est?
felix, qui quod amat defendere fortiter audet,
cui sua "non feci!" dicere amica potest.
Ferreus est nimiumque suo favet ille dolori,
cui petitur victa palma cruenta rea.
Ipse miser vidi, cum me dormire putares,
sobrius adposito crimina vestra mero.
Multa supercillo vidi vibrante loquentes;
nutibus in vestris pars bona vocis erat.
Non oculi tacuere tui, conscriptaque vino
mensa, nec in digitis littera nulla fuit.
Sermonem agnovi, quod non videatur, afentem
verbaque pro certis iussa valere notis.
Iamque frequents ierat mena conviva relicta;
compositi iuvenes unus et alter erant.
Inproba tum vero iungentes oscula vidi—
illa mihi lingua nexa fuisse liquet—
qualia non fratri tulerit germana severo,
sed tulerit cupido mollis amica viro;
qualia credibile est non Phoebo ferre Dianam,
sed Venerem Marti saepe tulisse suo.

Ovid

Amores II, 5 (1-32)

No love is worth so much—fly away, Cupid
with your quiver—that I pray often for death.
I pray for death each time I recall your affairs,
you girl born for my everlasting torment.
No smudged note informs me of your deeds,
nor the furtive giving of gifts that accuses you.
I wish that my lot were such that I could not win!
Wretched me! Why is my affliction so strong?
Happy is the one who dares to defend his love,
to whom his mistress says, "I did not do it!"
He is iron of heart and inflicts his own pain,
who wins a triumph by victory of the guilty.
I saw your guilty acts myself with a sober eye,
when the wine was poured and you thought
I was asleep. I saw you both say things with a
quivering of the brow; and through your nods.
Your eyes, too, girl, were full of speech and
you wrote all over the table with wine, never
missing a single letter. I recognized that your
speech was replete with secret messages and
your words were charged with special meaning.
And now the crowd of guests had departed and
there were only two boys left, drunk with wine.
Then I saw the shameful shared kisses, these
were clearly passionate kisses of the tongue,
not as those a sister would give to her brother,
but such as a yielding girl gives to her new lover;
not like the one that Diana grants to Phoebus,
but like the one Venus often bestows on Mars.

Amores II, X

Tu mihi, tu certe, memini, Graecine, negabas
uno posse aliquem tempore amare duas.
Per te ego decipior, per te deprensus inermis—
ecce, duas uno tempore turpis amo!
Utraque formosa est, operosae cultibus ambae;
artibus in dubio est haec sit an illa prior.
Pulchrior hac illa est, haec est quoque pulchrior illa;
et magis haec nobis, et magis illa placet!
Erro, velut ventis discodibus acta phaselos,
dividuumque tenent alter et alter amor.
Quid geminas, Erycina, meos sine fine dolores?
non erat in curas una puella satis?
quid folia arboribus, quid pleno sidera caelo,
in freta colelctas alta quid addis aquas?
Sed tamen hoc melius, quam si sine amore iacerem—
hostibus eveniat vita severa meis!
Hostibus eveniat viduo dormire cubili
et medio laxe ponere membra toro!
At mihi saevus amor somnos abrumpat inertes,
simque mei lecti non ego solus onus!
Me mea disperdat nullo prohibente puella—
si satis una potest, si minus una, duae!
Sufficiam—graciles, non sunt sine viribus artus;
pondere, non nervis, corpora nostra carent;
et lateri dabit in vires alimenta voluptas.
Decepta est opera nulla puella mea;
saepe ego lascive consumpsi tempora noctis,
utilis et forti coropore mane fui.
Felix, quem Veneris certamina mutua perdunt!
Di faciant, leti causa sit ista mei!

Ovid

❖

Amores II, 10

It was you, Graecinus, certainly, I remember,
who declared to me that it was impossible for
any man to love two girls at the same time.
To you I owe my fall, being caught with my
guard down; lo, I am now in love with two girls.
Each one is beautiful, both refined in their dress;
in their talents, it is doubtful which is the better.
The one is fairer than the other, the other is
fairer than she; one please me more, and so
does the other. I veer like a ship driven by
contrasting winds, and my love is now for
one, now for the other, it veers about and
keeps me in a state of constant confusion.
Why, lady of Eryx, do you double my woes?
Was not one love enough anxiety for me.
Why add leaves to the trees, stars to the
full sky, and more water to the deep seas?
And yet it is better than it I were without love
and alone—may such a life fall to my enemies!
To my enemies fall the lot of a lonely bed,
and the laying of loose limbs in their sleep.
But for me, let cruel love break off my slumber
and may I not be the only burden of my bed.
Let my powers be laid waste by love, and let
me say, if one suffices, then, why not two?
I shall meet the test—my limbs are slender
but not without strength; it is bulk, not sinew,
that my body lacks, and delight will feed the
vigor of my loins. No fair girl has ever been
deceived by me; often I have made love all
night long and reached morning fit and strong.
Happy is he the one who is laid low by love.
My gods, let my end come from such a cause.

❖

Ars Amatoria I (35-56, 61-66)

Principio quod amare velis, reperire labora,
Qui nova nunc primum miles in arma venis.
Proximus huic labor est placitam exorare puellam:
Tertius, ut longo tempore duret amor.
Hic modus, haec nostro sginibitur area curru:
Haec erit admissa meta premenda rota.
Dum licet, et loris passim potes ire solutis,
Elife cui dicas "tu mihi sola places."
Haec tibi non tenues veniet delapsa per auras:
Quarenda est oculis apta puella tuis.
Scit bene venator cervis ubi retia tendat.
Scit bene qua frendens valle maretur aper;
Aucupibus noti fructices; qui sustinet hamos,
Novit quae multo pisce natentur aquae:
Tu quoque, materiam longo qui quaeris amori,
Ante frequents quo sit disce puella loco.
Non ego quarentem vento dare vela iubeo,
Nec tibi, ut invenias, longa terenda via est.
Andromedan Persius nigris portarit ab Indis,
Raptaque sit Phrygio Fraia puella viro,
Tot tibi tamque dabit formosas Roma puellas,
"Haec habet" ut dicas "quicquid in orbe fuit."

Seu caperis primus et adhuc crescentibus annis,
Ante oculos veniet vera puella tuos:
Sive cupis iuvenem, iuvenes tibi mille placebunt,
Cogeris et voti nescius esse tui:
Seu te forte iuvat sera et sapientior aetas,
Hoc quoque, crede mihi, plenius agmen erit.

Ovid

The Art of Love, Book 1 (35-56, 61-66)

The first thing you must do is to find an object
for you love, you who now for the first time come
to fight in this new warfare. The next task is to win
the girl that attracts you; the third task is to make
your love endure. These are the limits of my field
where my chariot shall travel, this is the goal the
flying wheel of my chariot should touch upon.
While you are still free and can walk about in the
public with a loosened rein, choose a girl to whom
you will say, "You alone please me." She will not
come floating down to you through the thin air, she
must be sought, this girl whom your eyes approve.
The hunter who knows where to spread his nets
for the stag knows well in which fields the boars
with gnashing teeth are found; the fowler knows
which copses contain the birds and the fisherman
knows in which waters he will find the most fish;
you too, who seek the object of a lasting passion
must learn the places where the maidens haunt.
I will not advise you to set your sails before the
wind or that you must travel a long journey.
Though Perseus brought Andromeda from India,
though the Phrygian lover carried off a Greek girl,
Rome has so many fair maidens that you will say
"Here is all the beauty of the world."

Are you attracted by young girls still in their
ripening years? You will find such maidens here.
Do you prefer a full-grown beauty? There are
thousands here who will please you, and try
as you may you will not know which one to
choose. Or do you prefer a mature woman in
her later years? These too are quite numerous.

❖

Non est forma satis

Non est forma satis nec quae vult bella videri
debet vulgari more placere sibi.
Dicta, sales, lusus, sermonis gratia, risus
vincunt naturae candidioris opus.
Condit enim formam quicquid consumitur artis,
et nisi velle subest, gratia nuda perit.

Aurea mala mihi

Aurea mala mihi, dulcis mea Martia, mittis,
mittis et hirsutae munera castaneae.
Omnia grata putem, sed si magis ipsa venire
ornares donum, pulcra puella, tuum.
Tu licet apportes stringentia mala palatum,
tristia mandenti est melleus ore sapor.
At si dissimulus, multum mihi cara, venire,
oscula cum pomis mitte; vorabo libens.

Foeda est in coitu

Foeda est in coitu et brevis voluptas
et taedet Veneris statim peractae.
Non ergo ut pecudes libidinosae
caeci protinus irruamus illuc
nam languescit amor peritque flamma;
sed sic sic sine fine feriati
et tecum iaceamus osculantes.
Hic nullus labor est ruborque nullus:
hoc iuvit, iuvat et diu iuvabit;
hoc non deficit incipitque semper.

Petronius (circa A.D. 5-circa A.D. 65)

External Beauty

External beauty is not enough, and the
woman who wishes to appear fair must
not be content with a common demeanor.
Words, wit, play, sweet talk, and laughter
surpass the work of a nature too simple.
For the expense of art seasons beauty, and
naked loveliness is wasted in vain, if you
do not have the will to please another.

Golden Apples

You send me golden apples, my sweet Martia,
and you send the fruit of the shaggy chestnut.
I love them all, but should you choose to come
in person, my girl, you would beautify your gift.
Come if you will, and lay sour apples on my tongue,
the sharp flavor will be like honey as I taste them.
But if you decide not to come, my dear, send me
kisses on the apples, and I will gladly devour them.

The Pleasure of Love

The pleasure of love is gross and brief and
once love is consummated it often brings hate.
Let us not rush blindly into love like lustful
beasts, for love sickens and the flame dies;
but even so, even so, let us enjoy an eternal
holiday and lie with your lips next to mine.
No work is here and no shame; in this there
is only delight and will be so forever; in this
there is no end but an eternal beginning.

❖

Sit nox illa diu nobis dilecta

Sit nox illa diu nobis dilecta, Nealce,
quae te prima meo pectore composuit:
sit torus et lecti genius secretaque lampas,
quis tenera in nostrum veneris arbitrium.
Ergo age duremus, quamvis adoleverit aetas,
utamurque annis quos mora parva teret.
Fas et iura sinunt veterest extendere amores;
fac cito quod coeptum est, non cito desinere.

Lecto compositus

Lecto compositus vix prima silentia noctis
carpebam et comno lumina victa dabam,
eum me saevus Amor prensat sursumque capillis
excitat et lacerum pervigilare iubet.
"Tu famulus meus," inquit, "ames cum mille puellas,
solus, io, solus, dure, iacere potes?"
Exsilio et pedibus nudis tunicaque soluta
omne iter ingredior, nullum iter expedio.
Nunc propero, nunc ire piget, rursumque redire
paenitet, et pudor est stare via media.
Ecce tacent voces hominum strepitusque viarum
et volucrum cantus fidaque turba canum;
solus ego ex cunctis paveo somnumque torumque,
et sequor imperium, magne Cupido, tuum.

Petronius

❖

That Long Night

That long night will be dear to us, Nealce,
when you first laid your head on my breast:
The bed, and the couch, and the silent lamp
that saw you come softly to do your pleasure
are all so dear. Come then, let us endure even
though we have grown older and enjoy these
years which will soon pass. It is quite proper
to prolong our love as we grow old. Grant that
what we began in such haste, not end in haste.

At Rest in Bed

I had just gone to bed and begun to enjoy the silence
of the night and sleep was slowly overcoming my eyes.
When savage Love jerked me up by the hair and threw
me about and commanded me to stay up all the night.
He said, "You are my slave, the lover of a thousand
girls, have you become so tough that you can lie
here all alone?" I jumped up in my barefeet and got
half dressed and ran off in all directions, and went
nowhere by any of them. First I ran, then I lingered
and I am now ashamed to be wandering the streets.
The voice of men, the roar of carts, the songs of birds,
even the barking of the dogs, everything was still, and
me alone, afraid of my bed and sleep, ruled by lust.

❖

Satires, VI

Nota bonae secreta deae, cum tibia lumbos
incitat et cornu pariter vinoque feruntur
attonitae crinemque rotant ululantque Priapi
maenades. I quantus tunc illis mentibus ardor
concubitus, quae vox saltante libidine, quantus
ille meri veteris per crura madentia torrens!
Lenonum ancillas posita Saufeia corona
provocat ac tollit pendentis praemia coxae;
ipsa Medullinae fluctum crisantis adorat:
palma inter dominas, virtus natalibus aequa.
Nil ibi per ludum simulabitur, omnia fient
ad verum, quibus incendi iam frigidus aevo
Laomedontiades et Nestoris hirnea possit.
Tunc prurigo morae inpatiens, tum femina simplex,
ac pariter toto repetitus clamor ab antro
"iam fas est, admitte viros." Si domit adulter,
illa iubet sumpto iuvenem properare cucullo;
si nihil est, servis incurritur; abstuleris spem
servorum, veniet conductus aquarius; hic si
quaeritur et desunt homines, mora nulla per ipsam,
quo minus imposito clunem summittat asello.
Atque utinam ritus veteres et publica saltem
his intacta malis agerentur sacra! Sed omnes
noverunt Mauri atque Indi quae psaltria penem
maiorem, quam sunt duo Caesaris Anticatones,
illuc, testiculi sibi conscius unde fugit mus,
intulerit, ubi velari pictura iubetur
quaecumque alterius sexus imitata figuras.

Juvenal (circa 60-circa 140)

❖

Satires, Book 6

Well known are the mysteries of the secret goddess, when the flute incites the loins and the Maenads of Priapus dance along in a frenzy of music and wine, whirling their heads and howling. What primal urges burn within their breast! What cries they utter as the passion surges within! How they drench themselves in wine! Saufeia challenges the slaves girl to a contest. She wins the contest but she has to bow to the knee of Medullina. There is no pretence in the game; they play their roles in a manner that would warm the cold blood of Priam or Nestor. Now their impatient desire can wait no longer, and woman shows her true nature, and the cry comes from every corner, "Now we can act, let in the men!" If one youth is asleep, another is called to put on his clothes and hurry along; if they can find no one else, the women will find the slaves; if these fail too, they will fetch a water-carrier. What a shame that our ancient rituals and public rites are polluted by orgies such as these! But every Moor and Indian knows the lute player who brought all the men into a yard bigger than Anticatos of Caesar where every mouse struts about proud of his virility, and where every picture of the male form is veiled.

❖

Pervigilium Veneris (1-25)

Cras amet qui nunquam amavit quique amavit cras amet:
Ver novum, ver iam canorum, ver renatus orbis est;
Vere concordant amores, vere nubunt alites,
Et nemus comam resolvit de maritis imbribus.
Cras amet qui nunquam amavit quique amavit cras amet.

Cras amorum copulatrix inter umbras arborum
Inplicat casas virentes de flagello myrteo:
Cras canoris feriatos ducit in silvis choros;
Cras Dione iura dicit fulta sublimi throno.
Cras amet qui nunquam amavit quique amavit cras amet.

Cras erit cum primus aether copulavit nuptias;
Tunc cruore de supermo et ponti globo,
Caerulas inter catervas, inter et bipedes equos,
Fecit undantem Dionem de maritis imbribus.
Cras amet qui nunquam amavit quique amavit cras amet.

Ipsa gemmis purpurantem pingit annum floridis;
Ipsa turgentes papillas de Favoni spiritu
Urget in nodod tepentes; ipsa roris lucidi,
Noctis aura quem relinquit, spargit umentes aquas.
Cras amet qui nunquam amavit quique amavit cras amet.

Emicant lacrimae trementes de caduco pondere,
Gutta praeceps orbe parvo sustinet casus suos:
Umor ille quem serenis astra rorant noctibus
Mane virgines papillas solvit umenti peplo.
Cras amet qui nunquam amavit quique amavit cras amet.

Anonymous (circa 300)

❖

The Vigil of Venus (1-25)

Who has not loved by tomorrow's dawn shall love.
For spring is new and full of song, spring brings new life,
In spring the song birds love to mate and sing together,
The forest unfold its tender leaves in the renewing rain,
And those without love shall love by tomorrow's dawn.

Tomorrow the queen of love under the forest's shade
Shall join fair lovers with the boughs of myrtle trees.
Tomorrow she leads her chorus in song and dance
Tomorrow Dione shall rule from her sublime throne.
Who has not loved shall love by tomorrow's dawn.

Tomorrow when the air has mingled with primal light
And the celestial foam is joined with the mystic sea,
With dolphins and porpoises and other sea creatures
Dione shall be courted as a bride beneath the waves.
Who has not loved shall love by tomorrow's dawn.

Her shining light paints the year with new blossoms,
The Favonian wind makes a young man's heart flutter
Soft as the glistening mist falling on a veil of twilight
And scatters the fragrance of dew on flowing waters.
Who has not loved shall love by tomorrow's dawn.

The heavy tears well up, each drop a falling sphere,
That bears within a tiny world the hope of new love.
The serene vapours from stars deep in a quiet night
Loosens the virgin buds from the mantle of dawn.
Who has not loved shall love by tomorrow's dawn.

❖

Veris dulcis in tempore

Veris dulcis in tempore
florenti state sub arbore
Iuliana cum sorore.
    Dulcis amor!

Ref. Qui te caret hoc tempore fit vilior.

Ecce florescunt arbores,
lascive canunt volucres;
inde tepescunt virgines.
    Dulcis amor!

Ecce florescunt lilia
et virgines dant agmina
summo deorum carmina.
    Dulcis amor!

Si tenerem, quam cupio,
in nemore sub folio
oscularer cum gaudio.
    Dulcis amor!

Carmina Burana (circa 1150)

❖

Juliana by the Greenwood Tree

One sweet spring Juliana
stood under the greenwood tree
in the company of the sister
Sweet love!

Who could pass you by at such a time!

The trees blossom now
and the birds lasciviously sing,
virgins' pure thoughts take flight.
Sweet love!

The lilacs bloom again
and the maidens in the vale
sing of the high god's power.
Sweet love!

Could I embrace the one I love,
and underneath the forest's leaves
I would kiss her with such pleasure.
Sweet love!

❖

Exiit diluculo

Exiit diluculo
rustica pella
cum grege, cum baculo
cum lana novella

Sunt in grege parvulo
ovis et asella
vitula cum vitulo
caper et capella.

Conspexit in cespite
scholarem sedere:
"quid tu facis, domine?
veni mecum ludere."

Carmina Burana

❖

Farmer's Daughter

The farmer's daughter
arose early at dawn,
with her flock and her crook
took some wool to be spun.

She had in her flock
a sheep and a billy-goat
and a bull and a heifer.
An ass and a nanny-goat.

She saw a scholar sitting
underneath the tree.
"What are you doing, sir?
Come and play with me."

❖

Tempus accedit floridum

Tempus accedit floridum,
hiems discedit temere;
omne, quod fuit aridum,
germen suum vult gignere.
Quamdiu modo vixeris,
semper letare, iuvenis, quia nescis cum deperis!

Prata iam rident omnia
est dulce flores carpere;
sed nox donat his somnia,
qui semper vellent ludere.
Ve, ve, miser quid faciam?
Venus michi subvenias, tuam iam colo gratiam.

Plangit cor meum misere,
quia caret solacio;
si velles, hoc cognoscere
bene posses, ut sentio.
O tu virgo pulcherrima,
si non audis me miserum, michi mors est asperrima!

Dulcis appares omnibus,
sed es michi dulcissima;
tu pre cunctis virginibus
incedis ut castissima.
O tu mitis considera!
Nam pro te gemitus, passus sum et suspiria.

Carmina Burana

❖

Coming of Summer

The season of flowers is here
and winter is clearly waning
and everything that was once bare
comes struggling back to life again.
My boy, as you go down life's road
be grateful that you never knew
how cruelly love can treat you.

The meadow beams gay laughter
of sweet flowers to be gathered,
But night will soon bring sleep
and dreams of unrequited desire.
Alas, what else is there to do
but turn to you Lady Venus?
Grant me your eternal grace.

My heart weeps in discontent
and no solace is to be found
I know your generous consent
is all I need to quell my grief.
Sweet virgin, the most lovely,
if you should hear and not heed
my wish, then death shall come.

You are delectable to everyone
but most delectable to me alone.
No other girl can compare to you
and boast of such virgin purity.
Consider me with kindness, for
your sake alone I sigh, I suffer
and I experience such sadness.

❖

Nobilis, precor

Nobilis, mei miserere, precor!
Tua facies ensis est, quo necor,
nam medullitus amat meum te cor:
  Subveni!

Amor improbus omnia superat.
  Subveni!

Comae sperulas tuae eliciunt,
cordi sedulas flammas adiciunt;
hebet animus, vires deficiunt:
  Subveni!

Amore improbus omnia superat.
  Subveni!

Odor roseus spirat a labiis;
speciosior pre cunctis filiis,
melle dulcior, pulchrior liliis,
  Subveni!

Amor improbus omnia superat.
  Subveni!

Decor prevalet candori etheris.
Ad pretorium presentor Veneris.
Ecce pereo, si non subveneris!
  Subveni!

Amor improbus omnia superat.
  Subveni!

Carmina Burana

Gracious Lady Have Pity!

Gracious lady have pity on my misery.
The sword thrust of your beauty has
pierced me. My heart is taken captive.

Merciless love conquers everything.

The fibers of my heart are entangled
with your tresses, the fire burns close,
My soul is in distress; I am powerless.

Merciless love conquers everything.

Your lips have a fragrance rarer than roses,
You are lovelier than all girls I have known,
sweeter than honey, fairer than the lily.

Merciless love conquers everything.

Your beauty mocks the grandeur of heaven,
I present my humble plea at Venus's throne,
I must surrender my life unless you help me.

Merciless love conquers everything.

❖

Floret tellus floribus

Floret tellus floribus
variis coloribus,
floret et cum gramine.

Faveant amoribus
iuvenes cum moribus
vario solamine!

Venus assit omnibus
ad eam clamantibus,
assit cum Cupidine!

Assit iam iuvenibus
iuvamen poscentibus,
ut prosint his domine!

Venus, que est et erat,
tela sua proferat
in amantes puellas!

Que amantes munerat,
iuvenes non conterat
nec pulchras domicellas!

Carmina Burana

❖

Blossoming Flowers

Flowers blossom to their peak
and bedeck the world with colors,
and the grass becomes green again.

May young men, about to love,
hold in reverence and respect
the avowals they pursue.

Grant that Venus may hear
those who call upon her and
send Cupid to be present.

May she allow the young men
who are earnest in their quest
to succeed in finding their love.

Venus, even through old, but
always young, sets her shafts
to flights of love in young girls.

She arms all lovers for contest
but never hinders the boys nor
allows the girls to be harmed.

❖

Basium XIII

Languidus e dulci certamine, vita, iacebam
Exanimis, fusa per tua colla manu.
Omnis in arenti consumptus spiritus ore
Flamine non poterat cor recreare novo.
Iam Styx ante oculos et regna carentia sole,
Luridaque annosi cymba Charontis erat,
Cum tu suaviolum educens pulmonis ab imo
Adflasti siccis inriguum labiis,
Suaviolum, Stygia quod me de valle reduxit
Et iussit vacua currere nave senem.

Erravi: vacua non remigat ille carina,
Flebilis ad manes iam natat umbra mea.
Pars animae, mea vita, tuae hoc in corpore vivit
Et dilapsuros sustinet articulos;
Quae tamen impatiens in pristina iura reverti
Saepe per arcanas nititur aegra vias
Ac nisi dilecta per re foveatur ab aura,
Iam conlabentes deserit articulos.
Ergo age, labra meis innecte tenacia labris,
Assideque duos spiritus unus alat,
Donec inexpleti post taedia sera furoris
Unica de gemino corpore vita fluet.

Joannes Secundus (1512-1536)

❖

The Thirteenth Kiss

Faint from our sweet encounter, love, I lay
panting; my languid fingers play on your neck.
The passion was all consuming, my lips were dry,
I could hardly breathe, I saw death before me.
I saw the waves of Styx roll before my eyes,
I saw old Charon waiting on the far shore,
I was trembling in the bottom of my heart
Until your kisses brought me back to life,
And bid the ferryman to wait no longer
But sail back to the shore without me.

I was wrong, I do not mean without me,
I am but a shade in the land of the living.
The feeble soul that dwells within my body
Is a part of you and will forever strive to
Break away from its fragile abode and flee
To its own place in the company of death.
And were it not for your love, my darling
I would leave limbs to the care of darkness.
Come, let your lips join my lips and let
Us bring our souls together in one breath,
Until, as the passion ebbs and begins to flow
As a single stream of life from two bodies.

❖

Basium XVII

Qualem purpureo diffundit mane colorem,
Quae rosa nocturnis roribus immaduit,
Matutina rubent dominae sic oscula nostrae
Basiolis longis nocte rigata meis
Quae circum facies niveo candore coronat,
Virginis ut seris violam cum tenet alba manus:
Tale novum seris cerasum sub floribus ardet,
Aestatemque et ver cum simul arbor habet.
Me miserum! Quare, cum fragantissima iungis
Oscula, de thalamo cogor abire tuo?
O saltem labris serva hunc, formosa, ruborem,
Dum tibi me referet noctis opaca quies.
Si tamen interea cuiusquam basia carpent,
Illa meis fiant pallidiora genis.

Joannes Secundus

❖

The Seventeenth Kiss

As the red rosebud unfolds its dewy petals
When night begins to fade into rosy morning,
So do the lips of my lady welcome the day
Bedewed by me with kisses though the night.
As the cherry tree blossoms in white and red
After spring has gone but before summer appears
So do her cheeks appear as the new blossoms
Of snow-white violets held in a virgin's hand.
O miserable me! Your kisses burn my heart,
Why must I be forced to leave your side?
Let those lips remain like roses all day long
When evening brings you to my bed again.
But if another lover should seek your lips,
May your lips grow paler than my cheek.

❖

Elegia I

Pierides alius dira inter bella cruentet,
Vulneraque ingeminet saeva necesque virum,
Cuius bis fuso madefiant sanguine versus.
Hei mihi! Plus satis est quem cecidiise semel.
Nos puerum sancta volucrem cum matre canamus
Spargentem tenera tela proterva manu.
Sic ego: sic fanti radiantibus adstitit alis
Cum face, cum cornu, cum iaculisque puer.
Fallor, an ardentes acuebat cote sagittas?
Anxius in voltu iam mihi pallor erat.

Elegia II

Cara meum gelida feriit nive Lydia pectus:
Dicebam "flammis haec, puto, tela carent."
Nec caruere tamen; sub aqua latuere favillae,
Flammaque per venas stillat aquosa meas.
Hei mihi, securi qua declinabimus ignem,
Frigore duratas si metuemus aquas?
Frigore fax nata est, tolletur frigore nullo;
Sperandum simili de face frigus erit.
Sume pares ignes, miserumque levabis amorem.
Lydia, frigoribus semper acerba noces.

Joannes Secundus

❖

The Prelude

Let others sing of the cruelties of war,
all of the carnage and dying heroes,
who shed their blood twice for fame.
I want only one death. I would rather
write verses telling how Cupid draws
his arrows on me to prove his power.

Even as I spoke, the boy drew near,
with bow and arrows and his torch, his
wings were quivering bright in the sky.
I trembled and grew pale with frights,
for I thought I saw him sharpening
his arrows on a whetstone for me.

Fire and Ice

Lydia hit my heart with a ball of snow
and soon ignited a fire within my soul.
This was a most strange manner to
start a flame with this frozen water.
But so it was. How can I live at ease,
when I am trapped by such perils?
There is no cold to quench such a fire;
must be vanquished with another flame.
A mutual warmth is my only salvation;
Come now Lydia and burn with me.

LATIN QUOTATIONS & PROVERBS

❖

Amor gignit amorem.

Proverb

✣

Amor omnibus idem.

Virgil

✣

Amor vincit omnia.

Horace

✣

Amor magnus est.

St. Augustine

✣

Verbo dat omnis amor.

Ovid

❖

Love engenders love.

❖

Love is the same for everyone.

❖

Love conquers everything.

❖

Love is the great teacher.

❖

Love always deceives.

Nec sine te Venus fit laetem neque
amabile quicquam.

Lucretius

Illa quibus superas omnes, cape tela Cupida.

Ovid

Mulier cupido quod dicit amanti in
vento et rapida scribere oportet aqua.

Catullus

Id commune malum semel insanavimus omnes.

Virgil

Hoc si crimen erit, crimen amoris erit.

Propertius

Qui nolet fieri desidiosus amet.

Ovid

Without you Venus there is no joy in love.

❖

Take these arrows Cupid with which
you will conquer everyone.

❖

What a woman says to her lover should
be written in the winds or on the water.

❖

It is a common complaint, we have
all been in love at least once.

❖

If this be a crime, it is a crime of love.

❖

If one wishes to escape idleness,
let him fall in love.

❖

Amans iratus multa mentitur sibi.

Publius Syrius

❖

Si fuit errandum causas habet error honestas.

Ovid

❖

Difficle est longum subito deponere amorem.
Difficile est, verum hoc qualibet efficias.

Catullus

❖

Ubi amor condimentum inerit, cuius
placiturum credo.

Plautus

❖

Odi et amo. Quare id faciam fortasse requiris.
Nescio, sed fieri sentio et excrucior.

Catullus

❖

Audax ad omnia domina, quae vel amat vel odit.

Propertius

❖

An angry lover tells himself many lies.

❖

If I have sinned in love the sin has an excuse.

❖

It is hard to suddenly stop loving someone.
It is hard, but somehow you will succeed.

❖

Where love is the seasoning, the dish
will please everyone's taste.

❖

I love and I hate, why do you inquire.
I know not but it is so; I am on fire.

❖

A woman will do anything when she
loves or hates.

❖

Militat omnis amans et habet sua castra Cupido.

Ovid

❖

Amor animi arbitrio sumitor, non ponitor.

Publius Syrus

❖

Qui nimium multis "non amo" dicit, amat.

Ovid

❖

Amoris vulnus idem sanat qui facit.

Publius Syrus

❖

Nescis quid sit amor iuvenis si ferre recusas
immitam dominam coniungium ferum.

Proverb

❖

Utque viro furtiva Venus, sic grata puellae.
Vir male dissimulat tectius illa cupit.

Ovid

❖

Each lover is a soldier and Cupid has his own camp.

✣

We choose to love, we do not choose
to cease loving.

✣

He who often says "I love not" is in love.

✣

Love's wounds are cured by love itself.

✣

You do not know what love is young man if you
cannot bear a harsh mistress and a shrewish wife.

✣

As stolen love is pleasant to a man, it is also
pleasant for a woman. The man dissembles
badly, but the woman deceives much better.

❖

Credula res amor est.

Ovid

✣

Humanum amarest, humanum autem ignoscerest.

Plautus

✣

Dum nos fata sinunt, oculos satiemus amore
nox tibi longa venit, nec reditura dies.

Propertius

✣

Successare novo vincitur omnis amor.

Ovid

✣

Expertus dico, nemo est in amore fidelis.

Propertius

✣

Cum ames sapis aut cum sapias non ames.

Publius Syrus.

❖

Love is a credulous thing.

❖

To love is human.
To be indulgent is also human.

❖

As long as fate permits, let our eyes have their fill of love. The long night is on its way and day does not soon return.

❖

All love is vanquished by succeeding love.

❖

I speak from experience, no one is faithful in love.

❖

You are not wise when you are in love. You are wise when you don't fall in love.

❖

Non sum ego qui fueram. Mutat via longa puellas quantus in exiguo tempore fugit amor.

Propertius

✣

Pauperas me saeva domat dirusque Cupido sed tolerando fames, non tolerandus amor.

Varro

✣

Et rex misellus ille pauper amat habetque intus ignem acrem.

Varro

✣

Cras amet qui nunquam amavit quique amavit cras amet.

Proverb

✣

Deum qui non summum putet aut stultum aut rerum esse inperitum existumen.

Caecilius

I am no longer what I used to be to her. A long journey changes a woman; how much love has changed in such a short time.

✣

Biting poverty and cruel Cupid are my foes. Hunger I can endure, love I cannot.

✣

Both king and poor man love; each carries the consuming fire in his heart.

✣

Tomorrow shall be love for the loveless and for the lover tomorrow shall be love.

✣

A man who does not believe that Love is the greatest god is either foolish or naive.

❖

Vivamus, mea Lesbia, atque amenus
rumoresque senum severiorum.

Catullus

✣

Facilius in amore finem impetres
quam modum.

Seneca

✣

Qui amant, ipsi sibi somnia fingunt.

Virgil

✣

Aut amat aut odit mulier, nihil est tertium.

Publius Syrus

✣

Omnes humanos sanat medicina dolores
salus amor morbi non amat artificem.

Propertius

❖

Come and let us live, my dear Lesbia. Let us love and not fear what the old men may say.

❖

It is easier to end love than to moderate it.

❖

People in love imagine dreams of their own.

❖

Women either love or hate, nothing in between.

❖

Medicine cures all human sufferings, but the sickness of love refuses a physician.

❖

Utque nudis primoque cupidine tacta quid facit ignorans, amat et non sentit amorem.

Ovid

✣

Non veniunt in idem pudor atque amor.

Ovid

✣

Amabit sapiens, cupient caeteri.

Varro

✣

Tandem venit amor, qualem texisse pudori quam nudasse alicui sit mihi, fama, magis.

Sulpicia

✣

Amori finem tempus, non animus facit.

Publius Syrus

✣

Amor timere neminem verus potest.

Seneca

❖

Uneducated and unfeeling for the first time at the impulse of love, ignorant of what she does and knows it not.

❖

Modesty and love are not mutual concepts.

❖

Wise men love, others are mere lechers.

❖

At long last love has come, love such that, to conceal it would shame it more than proclaim it.

❖

It is time, not the mind, that puts an end to love.

❖

True love can fear no one.

❖

Amor patitur moras.

Proverb

✣

Amor tussisque non celantur.

Proverb

✣

Alius est Amor, alius Cupido.

Proverb

✣

Non potest amor cum timore miseri.

Proverb

✣

Si quis amat non laborat.

Proverb

✣

Si vis amari ama.

Proverb

❖

Love endures many delays.

❖

Love and a cough cannot be hidden.

❖

Love is one thing, lust is another.

❖

Love and fear exclude each other.

❖

He who does not love does not strive.

❖

Love if you want to be loved.

❖

Omnis levia sunt amanti.

Ovid

❖

Quis fallere possit amantem?

Virgil

❖

Vinceris aut vincis haec in amore rota east.

Propertius

❖

Amore nihil, mollius, nihil violentius.

Ovid

❖

Laus est amore mori, laus altera si datur
uno posse fui, fruar o solus amore meo.

Propertius

❖

Tu tamen amisso non numquam flebis amico,
fas est praeteritos semper more viros.

Propertius

❖

All things are easy for a lover.

❖

Who can ever deceive a lover?

❖

Either you conquer or you are
conquered by the wheel of love.

❖

Nothing is more tender, or violent, than love.

❖

How glorious to die in love, how more glorious
if the gods grant us enjoyment of one love. May
I alone have the total enjoyment of my love.

❖

Cry sometimes for your friends, though he is
lost; it is always fitting to love departed lovers.

❖

Omnia vincit Amor, et nos cedamus Amori.

Virgil

✣

Is poterit felix una remanere puella,
qui numquam vacuo pectore liber erit.

Propertius

✣

Fulsere quonam candidi tibi soles cum
ventitabas quo puella ducebat. Amata
nobis, quantam amabitur nulla.

Catullus

✣

Felix, quem Veneris certamina mutua perdunt.

Ovid

✣

Amare et sapere vix deo conceditur.

Publius Syrus

✣

Turpis amor surdus auribus esse solet.

Proverb

❖

Love conquers all things, let us yield to love.

❖

To win happiness with one's mistress, one's heart must never be disengaged. One must never be free.

❖

The brillant sun used to shine down on you when you went where your girl lived, loved by you as no other girl will ever be loved.

❖

Happy is he whom love's strife has downed.

❖

Both to be wise and to love is scarcely granted even to the gods themselves.

❖

A shameful love is usually deaf.

❖

Qui amat, tamen hercle, si esurit,
nullum esurit.

Plautus

✣

Quanto minus spei, tanto magis amo.

Terence

✣

Auro contra cedo modestum amatorem,
a me aurum accipe.

Plautus

✣

Qui regi non vult amor vincatur.

Seneca

✣

Errat, qui finem vesano quaerit amoris.
Verus amor nullum novit habere modum.

Propertius

✣

Quaelibet autem aspera facilia et prope
nulla facit amor.

Proverb

❖

He who craves food is no longer
hungry once he is in love.

✣

The less my hope, the greater my love.

✣

Show me a rational lover and I will
give you his weight in gold.

✣

Let the love which cannot be
controlled be overcome.

✣

He who seeks the limit of mad love is
wrong. True love knows no bounds.

✣

Love makes difficult things easy and
almost unworthy of note.

❖

Qui in amorem praecipitavit, peius
perit quasi saxo saliat.

Plautus

✣

Ita est amor, ballust ut jacitur, nihil
sic celere est neque volat.

Plautus

✣

Ad mala quisque animum refer sua,
ponet amorem.

Ovid

✣

Amor et melle et felle est fecundissimus.

Plautus

✣

In amore haec sunt mala, bellum pax rursum.

Horace

✣

Durius in terris nihil est quod vivat amante.

Propertius

He who falls headlong into love suffers
worse than if he had jumped off a cliff.

✣

Love is like a missile, nothing is so
swift in flight.

✣

To free himself from love, a man need
only concentrate on his own problems.

✣

Love is a mixture of honey and bitterness.

✣

Love has two evils, war and then peace.

✣

No life is harder than that of a lover.

❖

Nunc scio, quid sit, Amor.

Virgil

✣

Haeret lateri lethalis arundo.

Virgil

✣

Sine cere et Libero friget Venus.

Proverb

✣

Quisque amat valeat, pereat qui nescit amare,
bis tanto pereat quisque amare vetat.

Plautus

✣

Numquam Amor quemquem nisi cupidum
hominem postulat in plagas conicere.

Plautus

✣

Amantium irae amoris integratiost.

Terence

❖

Now I know what love is.

❖

The fatal dart of love sticks in her side.

❖

Love grows cold without food and wine.

❖

Blessed is he who loves, perish the man who cannot love, a double death to the man who forbids love.

❖

Love never hopes to trap anyone in his loose nets except those of loose desires.

❖

When lovers get angry their love revives.

❖

Vivo et morior pro quibus amo.

Proverb

✣

Ubi amor ibi fides.

Proverb

✣

Se negare est amare.

Proverb

✣

Mutuo amore cresco.

Proverb

✣

Amore sitis uniti.

Proverb

✣

Amor distantia iungit.

Proverb

❖

I live and die for those I love.

❖

Where there is love, there is faith.

❖

To love is to deny oneself.

❖

By mutual love I grow.

❖

Be united in love.

❖

Love brings the distant near.

❖

Odit verus amor, nec patitur moras

Seneca

✣

Quare, dum licet, inter nos laetemur amantes,
non satis est ullo tempore longus amor.

Propertius

✣

Qui amicus est amat, qui amat non utique amicus est.

Seneca

✣

Res est solliciti plena timoris amor.

Ovid

✣

Hostis si quis erit nobis, amet ille puellas.

Propertius

✣

Scilicet insano nemo in amore videt.

Propertius

True love despises and will not tolerate delay.

✣

While in the presence of each other, no time
seems too long for lovers.

✣

One who is your friend always loves you,
one who loves you is not always your friend.

✣

Love is a thing replete with cares and fears.

✣

He who will be my enemy, let him love women.

✣

One is blind once stricken with love's madness.

❖

Intret amicitiae nomine tectus amor.

Ovid

❖

Nec tibi nobilitas poterit succurrer amanti,
nescit amor priscis cedere imaginibus.

Propertius

❖

Nihil sit, quod studio et beneloventia, vel
amore potius effici non possit.

Cicero

❖

Et mihi quod nullis amor est medicabilis herbis.
Nec prosunt domino, quae prosunt omnibus artes.

Ovid

❖

In amore haec omnia insunt vitia, iniuria, suspiciones
inimicitiae, inidiciae, bellum pax rursum.

Terence

Love often enters in the name of friendship.

✣

Noble birth will not help those in love, for
love is blind to the fortunes of one's family.

✣

There is nothing that can not be accomplished
without affection and kindness, or rather love.

✣

The words of love do not respond to medicine
and the healing art is of no avail to those in love.

✣

There are many evils in love: suspicions, quarrels,
wrongs and injustices, but war precedes peace.

❖

Meminerunt omnia amantes.

Ovid

❖

Amans semper quod timet, esse putet.

Ovid

❖

Ecastor mulier recte olet, ubi nihil olet.

Plautus

❖

Namque est feminea tutor unda fide.

Proverb

❖

Mulieri nimio male facere levius onus est quam bene.

Plautus

❖

Mulier saevissima tunc est, cum stimulus odio pudor admovet.

Juvenal

❖

Lovers always remember everything.

✣

A lover always believes that which he fears.

✣

The woman with the best perfume is the one who has none.

✣

The waves of the ocean are more trustworthy than a woman.

✣

For a woman doing wrong is less burdensome than doing right.

✣

Nothing is more savage than a woman motivated by shame.

❖

Dicere quae puduit, scribere iussit amor.

Ovid

❖

Sobria grata parum, cum bibit, omne decet.

Propertius

❖

Qui amans egens ingressus est princeps in Amoris vias superavit aerumnis suis aerumnas Herculi.

Plautus

❖

Quis legem dat amantibus? Major lex amor est sibi.

Boethius

❖

Semper in absentes felicior aestus amantes.
Elevat assiduous copia largo viros.

Propertius

❖

Varium et mutabile semper, femine.

Virgil

❖

What shame forbids me to say, love
demands me to write.

❖

When my girl is sober, she pleases me a
little; when she is drunk, she delights me.

❖

The lover who sets out on the road of love with
no money is in for more labors than Hercules.

❖

Who can give law to lovers? Love is a greater law.

❖

Women's passions are more favorable toward an absent
lover; long possession often lessens the desire of a lover.

❖

Woman is forever fickle and changeable.

❖

Quamvis diducere amantes non queat
invitos Iuppiter ipse duos.

Plautus

✣

Felices ter et amplius, quos irrupta tenet copula
nec malis divulsus querimoniis suprema citius solvet
amor die.

Horace

✣

Nihil enim facilius quam amor recrudescit.

Seneca

✣

Non bene conveniunt nec in eunda sede
morantur, majestas et amor.

Proverb

✣

Non mihi mille placent, non sum desultor amoris.

Ovid

✣

Quid non speremus amantes?

Virgil

❖

Jupiter himself cannot separate two
lovers against their own will.

❖

Happy are those held by an unbroken bond
of love that will not be separated before death.

❖

Nothing grows again more easily than love.

❖

Majesty and love do not always agree nor
do they seldom abide in the same place.

❖

A thousand girls do not please me; I am
a constant person in love (only for you).

❖

What may we not hope for when in love?

❖

Mulier est hominis confusio.

Proverb

❖

Pejor odio amoris simulatio.

Proverb

❖

Mulieres duas peiores esse quam unam.

Ovid

❖

Nec mihi rivalis firmos subducit amores:
ista meam norit gloria canitiem.

Propertius

❖

Mi neque amare aliam neque ab hac
desciscere fas est.

Propertius

❖

Molle meum levibus cor est violabile telis.

Ovid

Woman is the source of man's confusion.

✣

Pretence of love is worse than hatred.

✣

Two women are much worse than one.

✣

No rival can take my love away; it is sure
and today's splendor will last forever.

✣

For me it is not proper to love another
or to leave the one I have now.

✣

My tender heart is subject to injury from
the light arrows of Cupid.

❖

Amor quaerit iuvenes ut ludant cum virginibus.
Venus despicit senes qui impleti sunt doloribus.

Carmina Burana

✣

Delectant etiam castas praeconia formae.
Virginibus curae grataque forma sua est.

Ovid

✣

Differtur numquam tollitur ullus amor.

Propertius

✣

Difficilis est temperare amores quod te
non putes diu usurum.

Tacitus

✣

Novi ingenium mulierum; nolunt ubi
velis, ubi nolis cupiunt ultro.

Terence

✣

His amor unus erat, pariterque in belle ruebant.

Virgil

Love seeks young men to play with maidens.
Venus hates the old who are full of sorrows.

✣

Even chaste girls enjoy being praised for their beauty; virgins often worry about their looks.

✣

Love may be delayed but not destroyed.

✣

It is difficult to be moderate in love when you do not think it will last a long time.

✣

I know the ways of women; when you want to, they don't; when you don't want to, they do.

✣

Between them was a mutual love and together they were anxious to plunge into the battle.